RELEASING RELATIONSHIP BAGGAGE

CARLA YOUNGBLOOD

Releasing Relationship Baggage

BY CARLA YOUNGBLOOD

© Copyright 2015 by Carla D. Youngblood
Simply Carla
7255 Sawmill Branch Road
Windsor Mill, MD 21244
www.designingwithcarla.com

Library of Congress Cataloging-in-Publication Data
Youngblood, Carla Denise (Carla Denise Youngblood), 1958- .
Releasing Relationship Baggage/ Carla Denise Youngblood.—
1st ed p.cm.
Summary: Every relationship whether family, personal, or professional leaves a bit of baggage with us. The key is discovering how to hold onto that which helps us grow and release the baggage that no longer serves purpose.
ISBN 978-0-9861995-1-6
Personal Development- Motivation, Spiritual & Inspiration.

All rights reserved. No part of this publication may be reproduced or transmitted in any form or by any means, electronic or mechanical, including photocopying, recording, or by any information storage and retrieval system, without the prior written permission from the publisher or the author. Contact the publisher for information on foreign rights.

ISBN: 978-0-9861995-1-6
PRINTED IN THE UNITED STATES OF AMERICA

Contents

Foreword	5
Acknowledgements	7
Introduction	9
One: Family Patterns	13
Two: Balance in Relationships	17
Three: The Self Relationship	21
Four: The Covenant Relationship	25
Five: The Relationship of Giving & Receiving	29
Six: Relationship Chatter	33
Seven: The Relationship Dance	37
Eight: Expectations	43
Nine: Courage	49
Conclusion	53

Forward

He that walketh with wise men shall be wise: but a companion of fools shall be destroyed. *Proverbs 13:20*

When I was asked to write the forward for this book by Carla I initially was honored, then nervous. What do I know about relationships? After praying it became clear, everything we do in our lives is either because of, about, or designed to create or influence relationships.

In my own life, I have known for years the importance of nurturing and maintaining relationships. And like Carla, as a Preacher's kid, I have also learned when relationships need to be managed or they can derail you and those around you. This became even more obvious in every facet of my life; whether I served in the military, worked in corporate America, married, had children, once we began in ministry and our businesses.

As you read this book, I want you to know how I have been blessed by the relationship my family and I share with Carla. You will discover what I have had the pleasure to personally learn. This is a woman who has been through the trials, the ups and downs, of the relationship rollercoaster and is better for it. She has an incredible heart, and willingly gives you her sound advice. What you will discover in this book are situations Carla has experienced. She is sharing these experiences with you as valuable nuggets to help you learn how to recognize not only the actions and intentions of the people you are in relationships with, but how you own and are empowered to make the necessary changes in you to have the relationships you desire. Like Carla covers in the Chapter 3, you have to have an understanding of yourself before you can have a successful relationship with others. If you follow the wise advice in this book you are sure to see a transformation in all your relationships!

It is my honor to present to you Carla D. Youngblood. My hope is you will be blessed by her wisdom and counsel as much as I have continually been throughout my life. Take your time and let her wisdom and knowledge soak. God bless.

James R. Cooper, Pastor, Restoration International Christina Ministries Author, Speaker, Businesses and Personal Development Strategist

Acknowledgements

To my family who were my "first" teachers on relationships. You gave me what you had and it helped me to launch my journey into defining what a healthy relationship is. To my son, Darnel L. Youngblood I, my first and forever love relationship with a child. You are my greatest lesson in learning how to love someone unconditionally. I could not have had a better teacher.

The love of my mother, Sarah L. Youngblood and father Moses Youngblood, is a constant reminder of the need to stay connected to my faith. Thank you for your love and support to my sister, Colette and my brothers, Richard and Duane , I love you all to life. I am grateful for the guidance from my writing coach and the woman who helped me bring life to my Simply Carla series to life, author Regyna Cooper and her team. Thank you for believing in me, when all I had was a word from God. You are my forever friend.

Thank you to my friend and brother in Christ, James Cooper, author of From Crackers to Caviar, for agreeing to write my foreword. His voice was necessary in this book as we move towards developing a greater awareness of who we are called to be. He is a gift to the world.

Thank you to all my family, friends and supporters some who were in my life for a season, reason and lifetime. You were all my teachers on the road to Releasing Relationship Baggage.

Introduction

As I was preparing to write this book, I took a one week break between my writing projects to process my emotions. I needed to process the topic of relationships from a place that was not filled solely with my emotions. Relationships hold a very important place in my life. I come from a family of relational people who care about people regardless of what situation they may find themselves. We never meet a stranger.

I love this about us and at the same time it has given me a false sense of relationships. We missed out on the place where we must expect to receive unconditional love as much as we give it. This is where my story on relationships begins and why this book is entitled, "Releasing Relationship Baggage".

I have on many occasions settled for less in my relationships, without once thinking about the consequences of not having my own needs met. I convinced myself, I only had to give and it would be reciprocated. I was in for a rude awakening.

That may have been true in some circumstances. However, I know I needed to learn how to ask for what I want.

My journey to healthy relationships came through my ability to learn how to release people, places and things that were not for my good. Love without boundaries can become abuse. I had to be willing to suffer loss so that I could gain what I really wanted in my life. Growing up I always felt I was loved simply because I had nothing else to compare it to. Once I experienced what I call abuse, I knew my relationships would forever take on a different meaning.

The releasing of baggage in relationships requires we become clear about what we need on our relationships. My journey begins by getting clear on what I need in order to be in a healthy relationship. My greatest lessons came from being in unhealthy places within myself. My thoughts had to become clear about what made relationships healthy for me, based solely on my needs and ability to ask for what I wanted. In this book, I will share with you types of relationships I have experienced and the journey to understanding myself better though them.

At the end of each chapter you will be able to share your own journal notes.

Chapter One: Family Patterns

I have never given much thought to the relationship pattern of my family. Since preparing to write this book I have thought of nothing else. It is easy to assume that because your family bonds with people a certain type of way, then all families are the same way. The truth is all families have a relationship pattern. The pattern is designed to give you a start in life. It causes us to be drawn to certain types of people. In my family we have a loving, giving accepting pattern with people. We say it is based on our faith or belief system.

We never meet a stranger or found it hard to love on others. We have often sacrificed ourselves for the good of others. While I love how we relate to others, it gave me a false sense about relationships in general. Your family pattern can be misguided and set you up for unhealthy expectations.

It has never been a problem for me to give, my issue was being able to receive. It bothered me when I found myself in the company of needy people who were takers. Later, I found out I was attracting these kind of people into my life.

Growing up as a preacher's kid I thought that if you gave, God would make sure you received. While this is true to a point, receiving comes from the position of an expectation to receive.

All family patterns need balance. Healthy relationships are born out of the place where we learn this valuable lesson. Patterns not based on balance can leave you frustrated and without having your needs met.

I have lived a life story full of needy people. I don't blame them, because they did exactly what I allowed them to do. I take full responsibility for my inability to ask for what I needed from others. Realizing the need for health in your relationships will cause you to think seriously about how you are relating to others. I believe we teach people how to treat us.

If you want to know more about the people you are in relationships with, look at their family. If they don't have family around watch their behaviors. There is a pattern to how they act out their relationships. Most likely that pattern is the place where their comfort level exists within relationships. Getting to a place of balance will require a willingness to step out of the comfort zone.

Your family pattern is the place you revert to when your relationships are in crisis. Duress can make us lazy and fall into the familiar, unless we are willing create a new pattern of thinking and being. The good news is we can change these patterns. Our relationship with God is the one relationship that can help us to move beyond our natural tendencies or family patterns in our relationships.

Journal your personal notes about your Family Pattern:

Chapter Two: Balance in Relationships

There is NO such thing as measuring the balance in our relationships. When I speak of balance, I'm talking about having a harmonious relationship. Harmony means to be in agreement, to understand and to be in unity.

Harmony is what our relationships are in need of to be healthy. In a harmonious relationship you both give and receive based on your mutual agreement in your relationship. The process of being one in your relationship begins with being one with yourself. Without balance blame is inevitable. It is unhealthy to assume that other people are at fault because you choose to either be a giver or a taker.

The choice from a position of harmony is to always see the other succeed. When two people operate from the position of what is best for the other, harmony is inevitable and both parties win.

My desire to receive became a struggle in my marital relationship. It was a struggle because there was no harmony. Without harmony we both naturally retreated to our family patterns and comfort zones.

I believe all relationships exist to teach us something about ourselves. If your most intimate relationships don't create room for you to grow, you will eventually find a way out of them.

Balance requires honesty and making choices daily that keep you on the path to living a harmonious life. The ultimate goal is to find harmony within, so you can find external harmony. It also requires you set boundaries. Boundaries are lines you establish in your heart and mind so that relationships do not sabotage your life and peace. Boundaries help you to recognize when others are attempting to place demands and/or limitations on you that are unrealistic. Boundaries are necessary and healthy if you desire to live in harmony. It is the path to maintaining an emotionally healthy lifestyle.

Harmony with self is always at our disposal. We must be strong enough to ask for what we want and need. When we do, we attract those who are fit for us relationally.

Journal your personal notes about your Balance in Relationships.

___

Chapter Three: The Self Relationship

Everyone wants to be in a relationship. We all need relationships. Everything in life is based on relationships. The truth is until you get an understanding of your relationship with Self, a relationship with others is not possible. The relationship with Self is the answer to all relationships. When it is healthy, it leads to the understanding of relationships with others.

We can experience fear of being alone because we don't want to look at the place of void in our lives. We rush to fill it with a person place or thing. Fear threatens us because it knows that if we allow God to fill the void, life becomes less complex.

I've felt the fear of loneliness; it does not feel good. Fear does not want you to question your loneliness, you might find out the truth. It does not want you to confront the unhealthy places. As a matter of fact, fear gives you every reason why you should not confront those places. I have learned that the moment I made the decision to confront my fears, I am able to face what was keeping me from my true Self.

The truth is you can never get away from Self. It is with you everywhere you go. There is no way to avoid confronting your truths. Even when you don't confront them you are confronting them.

All relationships are designed to be healthy. We must remember our way back to health. When God designed us, he did so with a knowing on the inside of us. Our journey is to get us back to knowing, through the relationship of Self.

Journal your personal notes about the Self Relationship.

_____
_____
_____
_____
_____
_____
_____
_____
_____
_____
_____
_____
_____
_____
_____
_____
_____
_____
_____
_____

Chapter Four: The Covenant Relationship

A covenant is a binding agreement, a pact, an understanding. It is a promise to perform some action. We first learn of covenant in the scriptures, where God made a covenant with Abraham. (Gen 15).

The issues in our relationships usually surface, when we as women desire a more intimate relationship. Surface relationships in this environment rarely are enough. When we desire intimacy, we are looking for a more covenant way of relating.

Covenant relationships require a deeper level of agreement. The key to the covenant lies in agreement. This relationship is first experienced vertically, between God and man, then horizontally between man and woman. However, when we understand the impact of the first type of relationship between God and man, the desire for agreement will increase.

What I have learned from my own relationships is that unless there is mutual understanding and/or agreement, this relationship can never succeed. It will soon result in the breach of contract.

Getting two people to continually agree to do anything today seems to be next to impossible. It is because in today's society we all reserve our right to change our minds. In a healthy relationship partners continue to seek ways to agree, not to escape. Covenant requires transparency which will eventually lead to the transformation of the relationship. It is a shift in perspectives that always includes the agreement of the other person. Covenant always seeks to see that both parties win, even when it is not always apparent. It is a heart condition, an internal understanding that shows up in an external expression. A level of commitment you don't know you have, until it is revealed in your life. When you enter into covenant with the Creator you are well on your way to understanding the need for covenant in all other relationships.

Journal your personal notes about Covenant.

Chapter Five: The Relationship of Giving and Receiving

Staying in an unhealthy relationship without moving towards health is telling God you don't deserve his best for you. His best for you is his love for you. I remember telling someone years ago, I wanted a man to love me the way God loved me. She asked me if I thought it was possible. I believed it was, but my choices were not in agreement with what I believed. I had my doubts and because of doubt I allowed myself to settle for less.

Success in your relationships is based on your ability to see and know what kind of relationship you are in. if the relationship is not working for you, you must then exercise the presence of mind to do something about it. We must be able to freely communicate our needs and allow others to share their responses to our need. The success or failure of the give and take relationship is based on your continued search for understanding, clear communication and always choosing what is best for you. Relationships are always based on the part you are willing to play in them.

My relationship struggle with receiving was real. While being a giver is a great thing, until I learned the importance of being able to receive, my relationships were out of balance. I never felt like I was winning. I was giving my winnings away because I did not set an expectation for them. Without an expectation clearly defined there was no way for them to show up and if they did, I would not have recognized them.

My expertise on the give and take relationship comes from my observation of my family pattern. While we were known for helping many people along the path of life, we received little help on our own path. If you do this long enough people will begin to think you don't have needs.

They will show up in your life thinking you don't need anything because you appear to have it all together. Rarely if ever, do we have it all together. I later realized losing my voice (my truth) contributed to my inability to receive.

A healthy relationship is always about giving and receiving. It is the natural order of God's law. You do not give to receive. You do it out of the abundance of your heart with a proper understanding of God's order

When giving and receiving is working as it should in your relationships, it will produce a natural harmony.

Journal your personal notes about The Relationship of Giving and Receiving.

Chapter Six: Relationship Chatter

Chatter is the noise of life that will keep our relationships stuck in limbo, if we don't learn to quiet it. It is the rapid talking about trivial matters.

Chatter is designed to keep you away from the quiet life inside you. Chatter can keep you from being still and knowing. Chatter is designed to keep you from engaging with quiet time so you can come to a healthy relationship with yourself.

Those voices inside and outside of you will rage on until you learn to quiet the chatter. Relationship chatter is designed to keep you busy doing nothing, so you never succeed at accomplishing anything. Chatter is not only your internal dialogue; it is the noise of everyone and everything around you. The purpose of chatter is to keep you from experiencing relationship with your authentic self.

Chatter loves living on the surface. Surface living can keep you from expressing the person you were designed to be. You must confront chatter head on if you want to experience living from a quiet place. Stillness is the attribute that reveals the truth about your relationship with yourself. It teaches you how to be comfortable with who you are, without interference from those who think they know or don't know you.

Here are a few chatter attributes.

Chatter:

- Is known for getting you caught up in other peoples' business, gossiping

- Will lead you down an unhealthy road and when you come to yourself you have no idea how you got there

- Convinces you to make unhealthy choices because you feel rushed to make a decision now

- Presents a good case about why you should do something you know you should not be doing

- Blackmails you into agreeing to something you know you don't want to do

Chatter is designed to keep you distracted. Don't allow it to rule your life. Choose to come to the quiet place where that still small voice can speak to you and lead you to the relationship you desire to have with yourself.

Journal your personal notes about Relationship Chatter here.

Chapter Seven: The Relationship Dance

The ebb and flow of relationships are like a dance. There is a rhyme and a rhythm to the movement. Its sound is that of a sweet melody. The chords succinctly flow together, no matter the key or note. It requires you have an understanding of your own movement. The movement is orchestrated by the sound that resides in your spiritual DNA.

The dance is the beat of your authentic self that is encoded within you. It is your who and why. As you become clearer about your who and why, your movement sends out a distinctive sound in the atmosphere. Everyone who hears and understands sound knows it is you. You can't always hear the sound with your natural ear, but you know it by its movement in the atmosphere. It is frequency and to understand it, you must be tuned in to frequency.

When I got married I knew nothing about the relationship dance. We were dancing to the beat of different drummers. As I got clearer about myself, my movements became more pronounced. It became very obvious the dance partners were out of sync. For me, the sound became very unique.

I was dancing with an ebb and flow I did not know. I thought something was wrong with me. I lacked the necessary understanding about sound. It was something I was created to make from birth. The more I moved to the frequency within, the more obvious it became that though we were still dancing, somewhere along the way, we stopped being partners.

Dancing when not in partnership, over time will become a noise and chatter that irritates each partner. It is possible to believe you are in what you describe as an intimate relationship, only find yourself dancing to the beat of different sound.

This happens when the relationship ceases to flow according to the natural order. It becomes chaotic. The ebb and flow must always be a priority. When the rhythm is off, you must check in and reconnect the frequency to ensure that the relationship is still the priority.

Your unique sound is intended to be heard by those who understand and consent to the rhythm. If you are not moving together you are moving apart. The ebb and flow of movement is always realized in your ability to adapt to the sound and to move accordingly.

In the dance, someone must lead and someone must follow. You need to know your role and have communicated clearly your desire to dance your part.

When we spend time trying to imitate the movements of others, we can lose sight of our own movement. The sound is what dictates the movement. When not walking in your own frequency, it affects your hearing, which will them cause you to be off cue.

Our need for authenticity in our relationships lies in our ability to hear the sound and to keep moving. As women, sometimes we want to stop dancing until our partner shows up. Keep dancing, because when he shows up, he will know you by your ability, to move to the frequency that is in alignment with who he has been called to be with. Don't' allow the temptation to stop or move prematurely disrupt your timing and throw off your movement.

When we learn to be comfortable with our own movement, we learn it will eventually lead us to connecting with a dance partner who can understand the ebb and flow that is uniquely us. We can all participate in the relationship dance. The work lies in your desire to put in the practice and listen to the beat of your heart.

Shall we dance?

Journal your personal notes about

The Relationship Dance

_____
_____
_____
_____
_____
_____
_____
_____
_____
_____
_____
_____
_____
_____
_____
_____
_____
_____
_____
_____
_____
_____

Chapter Eight: Expectations

I came into my relationships with certain expectations. While expectations are good, they can be both realistic and unrealistic. I have experienced both. Some of my realistic expectations are to be treated with respect, honesty, and what I call basic human needs.

What I have learned is that all expectations deserve conversation. Without a conversation, you risk setting yourself up for being let down. Family patterns, life experiences and our own way of thinking and being about expectations can differ. The differences can have a major impact on your relationship.

Clear communication is the key to having or not having your expectations met. It is easy to assume your expectations will be met. But your assumptions may not lead to your desired outcome. At times I didn't want to have the conversation because I already knew the other person was incapable of meeting my expectations. In some of these circumstances, I would try to convince myself into thinking it did not matter. So I would forge ahead in the relationships only to be let down later. I would tell myself things like, you need to lower your expectations or trade it off for something else. Sometimes this worked, but most of the times it did not. When I stayed in relationships that were not able to meet my expectations, I got exactly what I expected, that lower expectation.

Fear will cause you to trade in an expectation, instead of accepting the fact and moving on to a place where your expectation could possibly be met. I have robbed myself many times in these circumstances. I was sending a message to myself that I did not deserve to have that expectation met. I've learned it's better to risk having the sometimes difficult conversation, even if it means compromise.

Not taking the risk of having an expectation met, is to tell yourself you are not worthy or deserving. You have every right to ask for what you want in your relationship. If it cannot be met then you have a right to stay or leave. Either way you must be clear about what you are compromising and be sure you can live with your decision. I'm not saying you should not compromise, I'm saying to make sure you can live with your choice.

You deserve every right to have your expectations met. Sometimes expectations come through exercising all of your options. It is a great way to ensure you are not carrying any extra baggage in your relationships. Sometimes we have picked up baggage along the way because we made a choice to settle someplace when we should have kept it moving.

Relationship expectations when communicated effectively can lead to a win- win for both parties. When we have the best interest of each other in mind, we seek to meet expectations or look for ways both parties can find common ground in our expectations.

Expectations based on our heart conditions are always designed to see that all parties have their relationship needs met.

Journal your personal notes about

Expectations

___

Chapter Nine: Courage

Courage is the attribute you must have if you are going to release relationship baggage and live the life you were created to live. I am consistently being challenged to practice it in my relationships. Courage is to do all that is in your heart from a position of truth. When you are allowed to operate in truth in your relationships, you are willing to take risks with disclosing your truth.

Courage will always show up where truth is desired. Relationships that require truth take courage. It is a strength I have learned to exercise in the face of what may have turned out to be a loss. It takes great courage to expose family patterns without making it personal and living in shame. Courage is the how to embrace a higher level of relating. Courage is your ability to share all that is in your heart without regret or judgment.

It takes courage to trust what is in your heart. I have learned how to embrace the act of courage through some degree of difficulty. It has come through trusting that God knows best even when I don't. Courage comes from the act of a conditioned heart that seeks to be unconditional. It seeks to walk in a manner that is true to self. There are no put downs in courageous deeds, it is an act of valor. Courage says I am taking this action so I can stay true to myself.

When we deny people their right to be courageous in our relationships, we tie their hands. We put a stumbling block in the way, which decreases the connection of our relationship. Courage is a teacher. Its best lessons are learned through somewhat difficult circumstances. You can't see the strength of it until you make the decision to go through it.

When we are courageous we trust the process to reveal truth. We become vulnerable enough to allow ourselves to go through life uninhibited by the thoughts/opinions of others. Fear is always present in the process. Courage responds by searching for a place where it can be true to itself. Your greatest relationships will be put through the test of courage.

The journey of releasing relationship baggage is led by courage. It is the place where God strengthens you and develops His character within you. This character trait is possible for all of us. It requires us to be willing to get off of the merry go round of a lack luster life and learn how to fly like the eagle which we were created to become.

Journal your personal notes about

Courage

In Conclusion

All relationships exist to show us how to change ourselves. We sometimes think they exist to change others, however when we do this we miss the point. Believe me, I have tried to change other people. It does not work. If you find yourself in this moment trying to change someone else, please know the person who is going to change is YOU. Changing you is the only possibility.

I began this book writing about family patterns. In my family there are many moments I can identify with as destiny robbers. But one moment in particular changed the course of our lives. It was the moment we knew we lost our voices.

It was a family destiny altering moment. My siblings and I both agree the courses of our destinies were impacted by this moment. We attempted to take an action and it appeared that the action caused us to be robbed of our destinies. What I realize all these years later is that a moment that seemed lost in time, was reserved for our future. It was a NOW moment reserved for some future date in time. It was our eternity invading now.

Most of the times when destiny moments happen, we are not prepared. It is because we have never experienced it before and/or we have no marker for how to move forward. Some of these moments simply require our obedience.

Those moments, though reserved for the future, are designed to create new family patterns. The value in destiny moments is to get you to embark on a future you cannot see. It is a place where we can acknowledge the present moment and prepare for the reality that is to come.

As the oldest sibling, my life has always been at the forefront of these moments. I was positioned to be in front to see what was coming. My role was to call those things that were not as though they were; to take the now moment and create the future reserved for some later date. That later date is now. It has come full circle and I walk in the totality of the work that began some 40 years ago. It is a finished work.

Each chapter of this book is a place I have found myself in as a result of emotional challenges. I needed to come face to face with each place if I was going to change the pattern of my life. I had to unlearn behaviors that served me no good and embrace new ones. Patterns exist and cycles are developed because of our inability to change our thinking. If we change our thinking we can change our lives.

The key is to learn which parts of the pattern are necessary for growth and development, and which parts have served their purpose. It is necessary to embrace new ways of looking at the patterns and develop them in a way that builds the future.

Releasing relationship baggage means something different to all of us. We must develop our own strategy for how we move forward in a healthy way. My hope is that you have been challenged to make changes within that show up without.

May you be able to release every piece of relationship baggage that no longer serves a purpose.

May you embrace new ways of thinking and being that can catapult you to the personal relationship destiny you deserve.

It's your TIME to RELEASE YOUR RELATIONSHIP BAGGAGE.

Simply Carla

Simply Carla collection is a series of pocket books designed to give you, the reader, easy to read reflections to assist with daily living.

Each book in the collection is a "fragment". This was an idea I had in 2012, taken from St. John 6:12. After feeding 5000 plus people, Jesus instructed the disciples to gather up the fragments that remain that nothing be lost.

Fragments are the broken pieces that we can lose sight of because they are small and can appear to be insignificant. Significance can be found in anything you choose to see as significant.

I love and believe in the power of journaling. Therefore in each book you will find a place to share your personal journal thoughts for inspiration and empowerment.

Carla D. Youngblood is a master life coach, marketplace ministry leader, speaker, and author. Drawing on her own life experience, Carla is an expert at teaching others how to bring order and structure to their lives and build a life in preparation so that they are able to meet any of life's challenges. As a preacher's daughter this ability comes naturally to Carla since she learned about spiritual discipline very early in life. Carla also conducts workshops and training sessions and has been a keynote speaker and workshop facilitator for women, youth groups, non-profits and governmental agencies throughout the country.

Carla is the executive producer of a blog talk radio show, *Designing Your Life*

With Carla. For more information go to www.designingwithcarla.com.

View a current selection of Carla's books on
www.designingwithcarla.com.

www.ingramcontent.com/pod-product-compliance
Lightning Source LLC
Chambersburg PA
CBHW050607300426
44112CB00013B/2110